Questions, Answers & Explanations

EASA PPL Revision Papers

Operational Procedures

Written and illustrated by

Helena B A Hughes

POOLEYS
Air Pilot Publishing

STOP PRESS – New UK CAA PPL e-Exams - The UK CAA are introducing new PPL e-Exams from October 2020. Rather than using paper exam sets, all the exams will now be taken online under controlled conditions. They will, however, still be taken at your flying school and under the supervision of an approved individual. Please note that the syllabus has not changed. By reading the Air Pilots Manuals and other reading materials mentioned in the books, and by testing yourself with the following test papers, you will be ready to undertake these new exams. The CAA has issued guidance for students taking these exams and this can be found by searching online for CAP1903G.

Copyright © 2020 Pooleys Flight Equipment Limited.

EASA Private Pilot Licence Aeroplane & Helicopter Questions, Answers & Explanations – Operational Procedures

ISBN 978-1-84336-209-8

First Edition published March 2014
Reprint September 2015
Reprint February 2016
Reprint January 2017
Revised Edition July 2017
Revised Edition September 2020

Origination by Pooleys Flight Equipment Limited.

Published by Pooleys Flight Equipment Ltd

Elstree Aerodrome
Hertfordshire WD6 3AW
Tel: +44(0)20 8953 4870
Web: www.pooleys.com
Email: sales@pooleys.com

AUTHOR

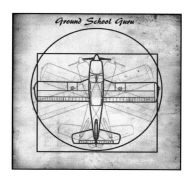

Helena B A Hughes

Helena Hughes was born into an aviation household, having her first informal "flying lesson" at the age of four. Her late father David was a flying instructor and also flew corporate jets. On leaving University Helena obtained her PPL. Shortly afterwards she started work in Air Traffic Control at London Luton Airport earning her Controllers Licence in 1990. Helena continues to be an operational Air Traffic Control Officer and is currently posted to Swanwick working "Thames Radar", "Luton Radar" and "Heathrow Special"; she is involved in controller training as both an Instructor and Assessor. Helena holds a fixed wing CPL/IR and has been a flying instructor since 1996. She also holds a PPL(H) and is a Radio Telephony and Air/Ground Examiner.

Helena would like to thank: Mrs. Brenda "Bedda" Hughes; Mr. Andrew Temple of Solent Flight Ltd; A Vrancken and H Ewing

INTRODUCTION

This book is intended as an aid to revision and examination preparation for those studying for the grant of an EASA PPL. Ideally its use should follow a period of self or directed study to consolidate the knowledge acquired and identify any areas of weakness prior to attempting the PPL examinations themselves.

The questions and answers in this publication are designed to reflect those appearing in the current examination papers and are set out in a representative format. No attempt has been made to replicate any actual examination paper.

Blank answer sheets are provided at the end of the book which may be photocopied to enable multiple attempts at each exam.

EDITORS

Dorothy Saul-Pooley LLB(Hons) FRAeS

Dorothy holds an ATPL (A) and a CPL (H), and is both an instructor and examiner on aeroplanes and an instructor on helicopters. She is Head of Training for a school dedicated to running Flight Instructor courses at Shoreham. She is also a CAA Flight Instructor Examiner. In addition, having qualified as a solicitor in 1982, Dorothy acted for many years as a consultant specialising in aviation and insurance liability issues, and has lectured widely on air law and insurance issues. This highly unusual combination of qualifications led to her appointment as Honorary Solicitor to the Guild of Air Pilots and Navigators (GAPAN). Dorothy is a Fellow of the Royal Aeronautical Society, first Chairman of the GAPAN Instructor Committee, and past Chairman of the Education & Training Committee. She has just completed her term of office as the Master for the year 2014-15 of the Honourable Company of Air Pilots (formerly GAPAN). She is also Chairman of the Professional Flying Instructors Association. In 2003 she was awarded the Jean Lennox Bird Trophy for her contribution to aviation and support of Women in Aviation and the BWPA (British Women Pilots Association). In 2013 Dorothy was awarded the prestigious Master Air Pilots Certificate by GAPAN. A regular contributor to seminars, conferences and aviation publications. Dorothy is the author and editor of a number of flying training books and has published articles in legal and insurance journals.

Daljeet Gill BA(Hons)

Daljeet is the Head of Design & Development for Pooleys Flight Equipment and editor of the Air Pilot's Manuals, Guides to the EASA IR & CPL Flight Test, Pre-flight Briefing and R/T Communications as well as many other publications. Daljeet has been involved with the editing, typesetting and designing of all Pooleys publications and products since she joined us in 2001. Graduating in 1999 with a BA(Hons) in Graphic Design, she deals with marketing, advertising, exhibition design and technical design of our manufactured products in the UK. She maintains our website and produces our Pooleys Catalogue. Daljeet's design skills and imaginative approach have brought a new level of clarity and readability to the projects she has touched.

Sebastian Pooley FRIN FRAeS

Sebastian is Managing Director of Pooleys Flight Equipment and a Director of Air Pilot Publishing. He holds a PPL (A). Sebastian is a Committee Member of the GANG - the General Aviation Navigation Group, part of the Royal Institute of Navigation and a judge for the International Dawn to Dusk Competition. He is a Liveryman of the Honourable Company of Air Pilots, a Fellow of the Royal Institute of Navigation and a Fellow of the Royal Aeronautical Society.

EASA PRIVATE PILOT LICENCE
– AEROPLANE –
OPERATIONAL PROCEDURES

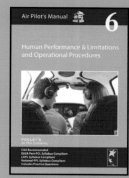

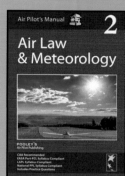

Before attempting these practice examination papers, you should have read the Air Pilot's Manual, Vol. 6 – Human Performance & Limitations and Operational Procedures and have completed the Progress Tests throughout the manual. In addition, you should read APM Volume 2, Air Law and Meteorology, Section 1, Chapter 9, Registration and Airworthiness & Chapter 13, Search and Rescue (SAR).

The Operational Procedures examination consists of 12 questions; the time allowed is 30 minutes. Each of the practice examination papers that follow contain 16 questions.

The pass mark is 75%.

Please read each question carefully and ensure you understand it fully before making your choice of answer.

Each question is multiple choice with four possible answers A, B, C and D. You should indicate your chosen answer by placing a cross in the appropriate box on the answer sheet.

Blank answer sheets are to be found at the end of this publication, these may be photocopied.

OPERATIONAL PROCEDURES PAPER 1

1. When a "light" aircraft departs from an intermediate position on the same runway following a "Heavy" aeroplane's departure, the recommended minimum spacing is:

    a. 2 nm
    b. 3 km
    c. 3 minutes
    d. 2 minutes

2. 4. In relation to Search and Rescue operations, the "distress phase" means that:

    a. Air Traffic Control has lost contact with an aircraft
    b. Apprehension exists as to the safety of an aircraft and its occupants
    c. An aircraft has an emergency situation
    d. An aircraft and its occupants are threatened by grave and imminent danger

3. An air accident occurring in the UK must be reported by the quickest means available to (UK):

    a. The CAA and AAIB
    b. The CAA and the Chief Inspector of Air Accidents
    c. The Chief Inspector of Air Accidents and the local police
    d. The Chief Inspector of Police and the CAA

4. You are flying by day and observe a ground search and rescue signal, to acknowledge you should:

    a. Fly over the site twice at a low height
    b. Rock the aircraft's wings
    c. Raise and lower undercarriage/flaps
    d. Rev the engine twice

5. Which of the following would be classed as an aircraft accident?

    a. A person on the ground is seriously injured after being hit by a component that has become detached from a light aircraft in flight
    b. A main tyre bursting on landing
    c. An aerial becomes detached
    d. A bird strike which slightly dents the leading edge of a wing

6. If making a flight in a single engine aircraft over water it is recommended that:

    a. Life jackets should be worn by all occupants when flying over water
    b. Life jackets should be carried for all occupants
    c. When flying over water beyond gliding distance of land, life jackets should be worn by all occupants
    d. When flying over water beyond gliding distance of land, life jackets should be on board for all occupants

7. An aeroplane's Certificate of Airworthiness:

    a. Is valid for the period specified on the certificate
    b. Will not expire under any circumstances
    c. Expires after ten years
    d. Is valid indefinitely, providing the aircraft is maintained, repaired or modified in an approved manner.

8. A PPL may carry out certain minor repairs and services,. Any maintenance carried out by a private pilot:

    a. Must be entered in the aircraft logbook if it relates to a primary control system
    b. Must be entered in the aircraft logbook and certified by the pilot concerned
    c. Must be entered in the aircraft logbook and certified by a licensed engineer
    d. Need not be recorded

9. The Airworthiness Requirements (BCAR Section A Chapter 6-2) allow for minor adjustments to be made to a control system while away from base. The second part of the duplicate inspection may be carried out:

    a. Only by the captain of the aircraft
    b. By an engineer licensed on the aircraft type concerned
    c. When the aircraft returns to base
    d. By a pilot licensed for the aircraft type concerned

10. A PPL may carry out certain minor repairs and services, these are:

    a. Listed in the Air Navigation (General) Regulations. The aeroplane concerned must be less than 5,700 kg
    b. Listed in the Pilot's Operating Handbook. The aeroplane concerned must be less than 2,730kg
    c. Listed in the Air Navigation (General) Regulations. The aeroplane concerned must be less than 2,730 kg and not used for public transport
    d. Listed in the Certificate of Maintenance Review. The aeroplane concerned must be less than 5,700 kg and not used for public transport

11. Any defects requiring maintenance which are encountered during a flight should be recorded by the pilot:

    a. On the Certificate of Maintenance Review
    b. In the Aircraft Technical Log
    c. On the Certificate of Release to Service
    d. On any handy scrap of paper which should be left in the aircraft

12. Before a flight, the legal responsibility to ensure that all of an aircraft's maintenance documentation is current rests with the:

    a. Pilot
    b. Aircraft Owner
    c. Aircraft Operator
    d. Chief Engineer

13. A BCF fire extinguisher

    a. Is only suitable for brake fires
    b. Is suitable for fabric fires and not really suitable for use in an aircraft cockpit
    c. Gives off highly toxic fumes when discharged and must never be used in an enclosed cockpit
    d. Is safe to use in an enclosed cockpit provided that the cockpit is subsequently ventilated

14. The safest extinguisher to use on a wheel (brake) fire is:

    a. Dry powder
    b. Water
    c. Carbon dioxide
    d. Hydrogen

15. Unless the flight manual gives specific contrary instructions, generically speaking in the event of a fire in the engine bay during flight, the immediate actions to take would be to:

    a.   Open the throttle and put the aircraft into a fast dive

    b.   Close the throttle, switch off the ignition and open the cabin heat control

    c.   Close the throttle, turn off the fuel and close the cabin heat and demister controls

    d.   Use the hand held fire extinguisher to attempt to put out the fire

16. A defect in the aircraft exhaust system may allow carbon monoxide to enter the aircraft cabin. Carbon monoxide:

    a.   Has a bluish colour and can be detected visually

    b.   Is harmless

    c.   Smells strongly of marzipan and therefore can be easily detected

    d.   Is colourless and odourless

END OF OPERATIONAL PROCEDURES PAPER 1

OPERATIONAL PROCEDURES
PAPER 1: ANSWERS

No.	A	B	C	D
1			X	
2				X
3			X	
4		X		
5	X			
6			X	
7				X
8		X		
9				X
10			X	
11		X		
12	X			
13				X
14	X			
15			X	
16				X

CORRECT ANSWERS: PERCENTAGES				
12	13	14	15	16
75%	81%	88%	94%	100%

OPERATIONAL PROCEDURES
PAPER 1: EXPLANATIONS

1. **(Answer: C)** 3 minutes.

    Wake turbulence departure separations:

Lead Aircraft	Following Aircraft	Minimum wake turbulence separation at time aircaft are airbourne	
Heavy	Medium, Small, Light	Departure from the same position	2 minutes
Medium, Small	Light		2 minutes
Heavy (full-length take-off)	Medium, Small, Light	Departure from an intermediated point on the same runway	3 minutes
Medium, Small (full-length take-off)	Light		3 minutes

    > FURTHER READING: APM VOLUME 6, OPERATIONAL PROCEDURES, CHAPTER 5 – WAKE TURBULENCE

2. **(Answer: D)** The Distress Phase is where an aircraft and its occupants are threatened by grave and/or imminent danger and require immediate assistance.

EMERGENCY PHASE	Definition	Duration
Uncertainty Phase	A situation wherein uncertainty exists as to the safety of an aircraft and its occupants.	Maximum of 30 minutes
Alert Phase	A situation wherein apprehension exists as to the safety of an aircraft and its occupants.	Maximum of one hour.
Distress Phase	A situation wherein there is a reasonable certainty that an aircraft and its occupants are threateneed by grave and imminent danger and require immediate assistance.	Until the aircraft is found and the survivors rescued, or it is clear that there is no longer any chance of so doing.

    > FURTHER READING: APM VOLUME 6, OPERATIONAL PROCEDURES, CHAPTER 6 – EMERGENCY AND PRECAUTIONARY LANDINGS

3. **(Answer: C)** When a notifiable accident occurs, the aircraft commander must inform:
    *   *The Chief Inspector of Accidents by the quickest means available and*
    *   *The local police when the accident has occurred in or over the UK.*

    > FURTHER READING: APM VOLUME 6, OPERATIONAL PROCEDURES, CHAPTER 1 – OPERATION OF AIRCRAFT

4. **(Answer: B)** By day the air-to-ground signal to indicate that SAR ground signals have been understood is to rock the aircraft's wings. By night the landing lights should be flashed twice, or if the aircraft is not suitably equipped the navigation lights should be switched on and off twice.

    > FURTHER READING: APM 2, AIR LAW & METEOROLOGY, SECTION 1, CHAPTER 13 – SEARCH & RESCUE (SAR)

5.   **(Answer: A)** An accident must be reported if, between the time when anyone boards the aircraft with the intention of flight, until all such persons have disembarked:

- *Anyone is killed or seriously injured while in or on the aircraft or by direct contact with the aircraft including anything that has become detached from it. This includes direct exposure to jet blast but not anything self-inflicted or due to natural causes. It does not include stowaways; or*

- *The aircraft incurs damage or structural failure other than any failure or damage limited to the engine or its accessories. If the damage is only limited to propellers, wingtips, aerials, tyres, brakes, fairings, small dents or small puncture holes it is not reportable. (Unless any of the afore-mentioned adversely affects the aircraft's structural strength, performance or flight characteristics and requires major repair or replacement).*

- *The aircraft is missing or completely inaccessible.*

FURTHER READING: APM VOLUME 6, OPERATIONAL PROCEDURES, CHAPTER 1 – OPERATION OF AIRCRAFT

6.   **(Answer: C)** The advice held in a CAA General Aviation Safety Sense leaflet recommends that when flying beyond gliding distance of land life jackets should be worn by all occupants.

FURTHER READING: APM VOLUME 6, OPERATIONAL PROCEDURES, CHAPTER 1 – OPERATION OF AIRCRAFT

7.   **(Answer: D)** EASA Certificates of Airworthiness are non-expiring, provided that the aircraft is modified, repaired and maintained in an approved manner. Aircraft governed by EASA must be maintained in accordance with a Light Aircraft Maintenance Program (LAMP).

FURTHER READING: APM 2, AIR LAW & METEOROLOGY, SECTION 1, CHAPTER 9 – REGISTRATION AND AIRWORTHINESS

8.   **(Answer: B)** Owners or aircraft operators holding a PPL or higher are allowed to carry out minor repairs or servicing on their aircraft. The legislation is set out in the ANO Article 16(7). Pilots should record any minor work carried out in the appropriate logbook and certify it with their licence number and signature.

FURTHER READING: APM 2, AIR LAW & METEOROLOGY, SECTION 1, CHAPTER 9 – REGISTRATION AND AIRWORTHINESS

9.   **(Answer: D)** In order for an aircraft to be considered airworthy again following any adjustments made to either the flight controls and/or the engine controls an inspection must be made by two licensed personnel, either engineers or inspectors. However, the Airworthiness Requirements (BCAR Section A Chapter 6-2) allow for minor adjustments to be made to a control system while the aircraft is away from base and for the second part of the Duplicate Inspection to be carried out by a pilot licensed for the type of aircraft concerned.

FURTHER READING: APM 2, AIR LAW & METEOROLOGY, SECTION 1, CHAPTER 9 – REGISTRATION AND AIRWORTHINESS

10.   **(Answer: C)** Owners or aircraft operators holding a PPL or higher are allowed to carry out minor repairs or servicing on their aircraft. The minor repairs and replacements permitted are listed in the Air Navigation (General) Regulations Part 4. The aeroplane concerned must weigh less than 2,730 kg and must not used for public transport.

FURTHER READING: APM 2, AIR LAW & METEOROLOGY, SECTION 1, CHAPTER 9 – REGISTRATION AND AIRWORTHINESS

11. **(Answer: B)** The Aircraft Technical Log is the place where a pilot may record any defect immediately following a flight. Subsequently an engineer will record the maintenance performed to correct the fault. Pilots should also review the Tech Log (as well as the Certificate of Maintenance Review and Certificate of Release to Service) prior to flight.

FURTHER READING: APM 2, AIR LAW & METEOROLOGY, SECTION 1, CHAPTER 9 – REGISTRATION AND AIRWORTHINESS

12. **(Answer: A)** Prior to flight it is legally the pilot's responsibility to ensure that the aircraft's maintenance documentation is current and correct.

FURTHER READING: APM VOLUME 6, OPERATIONAL PROCEDURES, CHAPTER 1 – OPERATION OF AIRCRAFT

13. **(Answer: D)** BCF extinguishers are suitable for use on all types of fire and so are commonly carried in light aircraft. The extinguishing agent is Halon. If it is necessary to use a BCF extinguisher in the cockpit all vents and windows should be closed before use, once the fire is out all windows and vents should be opened to clear the fumes.

FURTHER READING: APM VOLUME 6, OPERATIONAL PROCEDURES, CHAPTER 3 – FIRE OR SMOKE

14. **(Answer: A)** The safest extinguisher to use on a wheel (brake) fire is one containing dry powder. Their use is recommended for fires involving flammable liquids, gases and electrics.

FURTHER READING: APM VOLUME 6, OPERATIONAL PROCEDURES, CHAPTER 3 – FIRE OR SMOKE

15. **(Answer: C)** Generically speaking, in the event of a fire in the engine bay during flight, the immediate actions to take would be to close the throttle and turn off the fuel, this will mean the engine will run dry and stop. With no fuel in the engine or induction systems the fire should extinguish. Normally the ignition would now be switched off and preparation for a forced landing commenced. Throughout the procedure close the cabin heat and demister controls to prevent any noxious fumes entering the cabin. Note: your specific aircraft flight manual should be referred to for type-specific procedures.

FURTHER READING: APM VOLUME 6, OPERATIONAL PROCEDURES, CHAPTER 3 – FIRE OR SMOKE

16. **(Answer: D)** Carbon monoxide is a colourless, odourless and very dangerous gas. It will combine with haemoglobin in the blood more readily than oxygen and cause headache, dizziness, nausea, deterioration in vision, unconsciousness and eventually death. Defects in the exhaust system and/or heat exchanger may lead to carbon monoxide entering the cabin. Other engine exhaust gases do have an odour and may indicate that they, as well as deadly carbon monoxide, are entering the cockpit. Should this happen shut off all cabin heating and increase the supply of fresh air to the cabin by opening all vents and windows.

FURTHER READING: APM VOLUME 6, OPERATIONAL PROCEDURES, CHAPTER 3 – FIRE OR SMOKE

END OF EXPLANATIONS PAPER 1

INTENTIONALLY BLANK

1. Water contamination on a runway described as "flooded" means that:

   a. The runway is completely covered with standing water

   b. Extensive standing water is visible

   c. Significant patches of standing water are visible

   d. The runway is soaked and cannot be used

2. Operating limitations and information necessary to the safe operation of aircraft are available:

   a. Only in the pilot's manual

   b. In the flight manual and on placards and markings

   c. In the Airworthiness Review Certificate

   d. Appended to the Certificate of Airworthiness

3. In search and rescue operations, what does the following sign mean 'V'?

   a. Require medical assistance

   b. Proceeding in the direction indicated

   c. Request instructions

   d. Require assistance

4. The transponder code used to indicate an emergency is:

   a. 7700

   b. 7600

   c. 7500

   d. 7000

5. "The length of the take-off run available plus the length of the clearway, if available" is a definition of the:

   a. Accelerate/stop distance available (ASDA)

   b. Take-off run available (TORA)

   c. Take-off distance available (TODA)

   d. Emergency distance available (EDA)

6. An Alerting Service is provided:

   a. Automatically to all aircraft known to any of the Air Traffic Services

   b. To all aircraft for which there is a current flight plan

   c. Only by Flight Information Service Officers

   d. To all aircraft in receipt of an Air Traffic Control service

7. Which of the following would be classed as an aircraft accident?

   a. During landing the propeller tips are slightly damaged

   b. An engine failure in the circuit. Damage is confined to the engine and the aircraft makes a successful forced landing on the runway

   c. A person is seriously injured on the apron by the wingtip of a taxiing aircraft

   d. An aircraft under tow damages another parked aircraft

8. When flying over large bodies of water it is recommended that life jackets:

   a. Should be within easy reach
   b. Should be worn un-inflated
   c. Should be worn inflated
   d. Are not necessary unless flying more than 300 nm from the coast

9. During refuelling the aircraft and the refuelling station must be "bonded" using an earth wire. This is so that:

   a. It is obvious which aircraft is being refuelled
   b. The aircraft and the refuelling station have the same electrical potential
   c. The aircraft and the refuelling station have a different electrical potential
   d. The circuit is made and the counter can register how much fuel is drawn by that aircraft

10. Why should the cabin heat control be set to "off" or "closed" before engine start?

    a. There is no point selecting heat, as this will not function until the engine has warmed up
    b. To ensure all available airflow enters the engine induction to aid starting
    c. The statement is false and the position of the cabin heat control is not specified
    d. The system opens a way through the fire wall, it is closed in case of an engine fire on start

11. The following is a definition of what? "The length of the take-off run available plus the length of any available stopway".

    a. Accelerate stop distance available (ASDA)
    b. Take-off run available (TORA)
    c. Take-off distance available (TODA)
    d. Emergency distance available (EDA)

12. Which of the following is true in relation to the wake turbulence generated by helicopter?

    a. Helicopters only produce wake turbulence during hover taxi
    b. Compared to fixed wing aircraft of a similar weight helicopters produce more intense wake turbulence
    c. Compared to fixed wing aircraft of a similar weight helicopters produce less intense wake turbulence
    d. Helicopters only produce wake turbulence during forward flight

13. The strongest wake turbulence is generated by:

    a. A light aircraft at high speed
    b. A heavy aircraft at high speed
    c. A light aircraft at low speed
    d. A heavy aircraft at low speed

14. You encounter the following windshear on final approach: at 1,000 feet a 25 knot headwind component changes to a 10 knot tailwind component. What will the effect be on your aircraft's air speed?

    a. The air speed will remain the same
    b. The air speed will increase rapidly
    c. The air speed will increase slowly
    d. The air speed will reduce rapidly

15. What is the definition of "Pilot-in Command"?

    a. The person flying the aircraft
    b. The person authorising the flight
    c. The most experienced pilot in the aircraft
    d. The pilot responsible for the operation and safety of the aircraft

16. In the event of an engine failure during flight over water:

    a. Concentrate on getting the ditching right and do not make a distress call

    b. Ideally plan ditch into the swell and make a distress call as late as possible

    c. Ideally plan to ditch parallel to the swell, make a distress call earlier than if over land and consider selecting transponder code 7700

    d. Ideally plan to ditch parallel to the swell, make a distress call earlier than if over land and consider selecting transponder code 7600

END OF OPERATIONAL PROCEDURES PAPER 2

No.	A	B	C	D
1		X		
2		X		
3				X
4	X			
5			X	
6	X			
7			X	
8		X		
9		X		
10				X
11	X			
12		X		
13				X
14				X
15				X
16			X	

CORRECT ANSWERS: PERCENTAGES				
12	13	14	15	16
75%	81%	88%	94%	100%

1. **(Answer: B)** "Flooded" means that extensive standing water is visible.

    WATER CONTAMINATION ON RUNWAYS:

Damp:	The surface shows a change in colour due to moisture.
Wet:	The surface is soaked but there is no standing water.
Water patches:	Significant standing water is visible.
Flooded:	Extensive standing water is visible.

    The runway surface is assessed and reported to pilots in thirds – for example it may be described as being "wet/wet/damp".

REPORTING TERM	RUNWAY SURFACE CONDITION	NOTES
Dry	The surface is not affected by water, slush, snow, or ice.	Not usually reported to pilots.
Damp	The surface shows a change in colour due to moisture.	
Wet	The surface is soaked but no significant patches of standing water are visible.	Standing water is considered to exist when water on the runway surface is deeper than 3 mm. Patches of standing water covering more than 25% of the assessed area will be reported as WATER PATCHES.
Water Patches	Significant patches of standing water are visible.	Water patches will be reported when more than 25% of the assessed area is covered by water more than 3mm deep.
Flooded	Extensive patches of standing water are visible.	Flooded will be reported when more than 50% of the assessed area is covered by water more than 3mm deep.

    FURTHER READING: APM VOLUME 6, OPERATIONAL PROCEDURES, CHAPTER 7 – CONTAMINATED RUNWAYS

2. **(Answer: B)** The flight manual forms part of the C of A and specifies requirements, procedures and limitations relating to the operation of the aircraft. ICAO Annex 8: Each aircraft shall be provided with a Flight manual, placards or other documents describing any limitations within which the aircraft is considered airworthy, and any information necessary for the safe operation of the aircraft.

    FURTHER READING: APM VOLUME 6, OPERATIONAL PROCEDURES, CHAPTER 1 – OPERATION OF AIRCRAFT

3. **(Answer: D)** In search and rescue operations V means "require assistance".

    Standard Ground-to-Air Visual SAR Signals

V	**Require Assistance**
X	**Require Medical Assistance**
→	**Proceeding in this direction**
Y	**Yes or Affirmative**
N	**No or Negative**

    FURTHER READING: APM 2, AIR LAW & METEOROLOGY, SECTION 1, CHAPTER 13 – SEARCH & RESCUE (SAR)

4.   **(Answer: A)** The special purpose transponder codes are:

7700 = Emergency
7600 = Radio Failure
7500 = Unlawful Interference

FURTHER READING: APM VOLUME 6, OPERATIONAL PROCEDURES, CHAPTER 6 – EMERGENCY & PRECAUTIONARY LANDINGS

5.   **(Answer: C)** The Take-off distance available (TODA) is the length of the take-off run available plus the length of any associated clearway.

A clearway is a defined rectangular area of ground or water under the control of the appropriate authority, prepared as a suitable area over which an aeroplane may make an initial portion of its climb to a specified height.

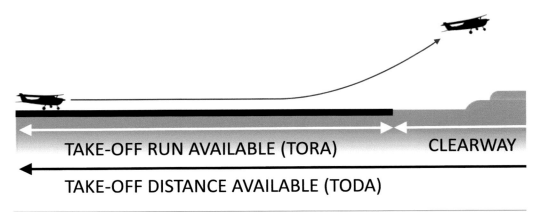

TAKE-OFF RUN AVAILABLE (TORA)   CLEARWAY

TAKE-OFF DISTANCE AVAILABLE (TODA)

FURTHER READING: APM VOLUME 6, OPERATIONAL PROCEDURES, CHAPTER 1 – OPERATION OF AIRCRAFT

6.   **(Answer: A)** An Alerting Service is automatically provided to all aircraft known to any of the Air Traffic Services. It means that the ground station will ensure that the appropriate organisations are alerted to aircraft in need of search and rescue aid and assistance is given to those organisations as required.

FURTHER READING: APM 2, AIR LAW & METEOROLOGY, SECTION 1, CHAPTER 13 – SEARCH & RESCUE (SAR)

7.   **(Answer: C)** An accident must be reported if, between the time when anyone boards the aircraft with the intention of flight, until all such persons have disembarked:

   - *Anyone is killed or seriously injured while in or on the aircraft or by direct contact with the aircraft including anything that has become detached from it. This includes direct exposure to jet blast but not anything self-inflicted or due to natural causes. It does not include stowaways; or*

   - *The aircraft incurs damage or structural failure other than any failure or damage limited to the engine or its accessories. If the damage is only limited to propellers, wingtips, aerials, tyres, brakes, fairings, small dents or small puncture holes, it is not reportable. (Unless any of the afore-mentioned adversely affects the aircraft's structural strength, performance or flight characteristics and requires major repair or replacement).*

   - *The aircraft is missing or completely inaccessible.*

FURTHER READING: APM VOLUME 6, OPERATIONAL PROCEDURES, CHAPTER 1 – OPERATION OF AIRCRAFT

8.   **(Answer: B)** When flying over large bodies of water it is recommended that life jackets are worn un-inflated. The advice held in a CAA General Aviation Safety Sense leaflet recommends that when flying beyond gliding distance of land life jackets should be worn by all occupants.

FURTHER READING: APM VOLUME 6, OPERATIONAL PROCEDURES, CHAPTER 1 – OPERATION OF AIRCRAFT

9. **(Answer: B)** During refuelling the aircraft and the refuelling station must be "bonded" using an earth wire. This so that the aircraft and the refuelling station have the same electrical potential, preventing the production of a spark which could ignite the fuel vapour.

FURTHER READING: APM VOLUME 6, OPERATIONAL PROCEDURES, CHAPTER 1 – OPERATION OF AIRCRAFT

10. **(Answer: D)** The cabin heat control should be set to "off" or "closed" before engine start because the system opens a way through the fire wall, it is closed in case of an engine fire during the start procedure. Not closing the cabin heat control could lead to poisonous fumes entering the cockpit should a fire occur during start up.

FURTHER READING: APM VOLUME 6, OPERATIONAL PROCEDURES, CHAPTER 3 – FIRE OR SMOKE

11. **(Answer: A)** The Accelerate/Stop Distance Available (ASDA) is the length of the take-off run available plus the length of any associated stopway. A stopway is a defined rectangular at the end of the take-off run available prepared as a suitable area upon which an aircraft can be stopped in the event of an abandoned take-off.

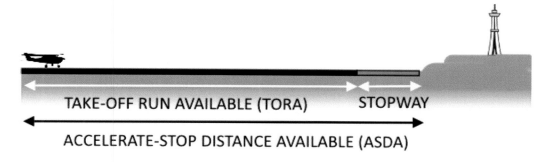

TAKE-OFF RUN AVAILABLE (TORA)   STOPWAY

ACCELERATE-STOP DISTANCE AVAILABLE (ASDA)

FURTHER READING: APM VOLUME 6, OPERATIONAL PROCEDURES, CHAPTER 1 – OPERATION OF AIRCRAFT

12. **(Answer: B)** Helicopters generate more intense wake turbulence than aircraft of a similar weight and size. To avoid, it is recommended that a distance at least three times the rotor diameter of the helicopter concerned is maintained.

    The wake turbulence is especially strong when the helicopter is hover taxiing, transitioning into forward flight and during its landing flare.

FURTHER READING: APM VOLUME 6, OPERATIONAL PROCEDURES, CHAPTER 5 – WAKE TURBULENCE

13. **(Answer: D)** The heavier the aircraft and the slower it is flying, the stronger the vortex.

    Wake turbulence is a by-product of generating lift. For fixed wing aircraft it is usually thought of in terms of the wing tip vortices, but wake turbulence is also created by the rotors of a helicopter. For fixed wing aircraft wake turbulence should be considered to exist from the time the nose wheel lifts on take-off until the nose wheel touches down on landing.

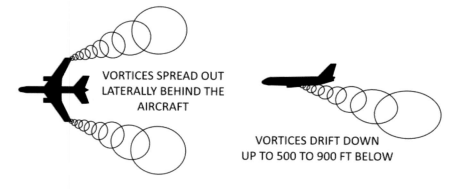

VORTICES SPREAD OUT LATERALLY BEHIND THE AIRCRAFT

VORTICES DRIFT DOWN UP TO 500 TO 900 FT BELOW

The intensity of wake turbulence increases with an increase in aircraft weight, as a heavy aircraft will need to generate more lift. Additionally, the more slowly the aircraft is travelling the greater the wake turbulence; therefore the hazard is greatest as a large aircraft is taking off or landing. For VFR arrivals vortex spacing is the responsibility of the pilot; however, the recommended distance will be given by ATC but not by FISO/Air Ground Communication Service. ATC will also apply timed separation to departures, but at uncontrolled aerodrome this too will be the pilot's responsibility.

Wake turbulence departure separations:

Lead Aircraft	Following Aircraft	Minimum wake turbulence separation at time aircaft are airbourne	
Heavy	Medium, Small, Light	Departure from the same position	2 minutes
Medium, Small	Light		2 minutes
Heavy (full-length take-off)	Medium, Small, Light	Departure from an intermediated point on the same runway	3 minutes
Medium, Small (full-length take-off)	Light		3 minutes

In general, vortices drift downwards, so flying above and to the upwind side of the lead aircraft's flight path can minimise a wake turbulence encounter. However, as you get closer to the runway lateral displacement has to reduced, so aim land beyond the point where the nose wheel of the heavier aircraft touched down. Vorticies are particularly persistent in clam conditions.

See also: CAA Safety Sense Leaflet 15.

FURTHER READING: APM VOLUME 6, OPERATIONAL PROCEDURES, CHAPTER 5 – WAKE TURBULENCE

14. **(Answer: D)** The airspeed will reduce suddenly. If the approach speed was 80 knots IAS, with a 25 knot headwind the ground speed would be 55 knots. Passing through the shear line results in a sudden shift to a tailwind, because of inertia the ground speed will change little, however the air speed will now be only 45 knots. A sudden loss of airspeed on approach will lead to an increase in the rate of descent, a rapid application of power will be necessary if the aircraft is not to sink dangerously low.

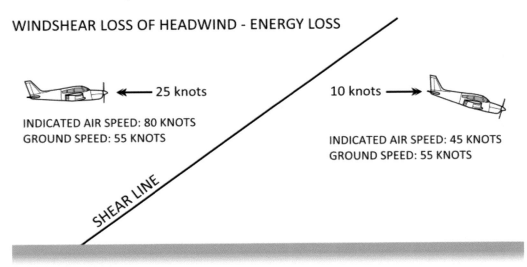

WINDSHEAR LOSS OF HEADWIND - ENERGY LOSS

◄— 25 knots

INDICATED AIR SPEED: 80 KNOTS
GROUND SPEED: 55 KNOTS

10 knots —►

INDICATED AIR SPEED: 45 KNOTS
GROUND SPEED: 55 KNOTS

SHEAR LINE

Windshear is defined as: Variations in the wind vector along the flight path of an aircraft with a pattern, intensity and duration that will displace an aircraft abruptly from its intended flight path such that substantial control input and action is required to correct it. Low altitude windshear is a particular hazard, that is windshear encountered along the final approach path, runway, the take-off or the initial climb-out paths.

The meteorological circumstances where windshear may be encountered include:
- Thunderstorms (both from the gust front and microburst),
- The passage of a front,
- A marked temperature inversion,
- A turbulent boundary layer

Additionally, topography or buildings can create substantial local windshear effects.

FURTHER READING: APM VOLUME 6, OPERATIONAL PROCEDURES, CHAPTER 4 — WINDSHEAR AND MICROBURST

15. **(Answer: D)** The pilot-in-command is the person responsible for the operation and safety of the aircraft and for the safety of all persons on board during the flight.

FURTHER READING: APM VOLUME 6, OPERATIONAL PROCEDURES, CHAPTER 1 — OPERATION OF AIRCRAFT

16. **(Answer: C)** Ideally plan to ditch parallel to the swell, make a distress call earlier than if over land and consider selecting transponder code 7700.

When planning a ditching the conventional wisdom is that the swell direction is more important than wind direction. From approximately 2,000 feet, the direction of the swell should be clear and your aim should be to touchdown parallel to the line of the swell and ideally to land along the crest.

If spray and spume can be seen on the surface of the water, then there is a strong surface wind. In this case it may be better to plan to land into wind, rather than along the swell. The best course of action is to aim for the crest again or, if that is not possible, into the downslope. The following table is reproduced from the CAA Safety Sense Leaflet 21 "Ditching":

WIND SPEED	APPEARANCE OF SEA	EFFECT ON DITCHING
0-6 knots	Glassy calm to small ripples.	Height very difficult to judge above surface. Ditch parallel to swell.
7-10 knots	Small waves; few if any white caps.	Ditch parallel to swell.
11-21 knots	Larger waves with many white caps.	Use headwind component, but still ditch along general line of swell.
22-33 knots	Medium - large waves, some foam crests, numerous white caps.	Ditch into wind on crest or downslope of swell.
34 knots & above	Large waves, streaks of foam, wave crests forming spindrift.	Ditch into wind on crest or downslope of swell. Avoid at all costs ditching into the face of a rising swell.

It is advisable to make a distress call earlier in your preparations to ditch than if the forced landing was taking place over land. Making an early call for help will increase the likelihood of being found and rescued quickly. It is important to be located quickly, survival times in cold water vary depending on water temperature, individual build, metabolism, fitness and the amount of clothing worn, but up to a sea temperature of 15° C is generally around one hour.

The sea around British coasts:
- Is at its coldest in March,
- Below 10° C between October and April, and
- Averages 5° C in winter and in summer 15° C.

Selecting 7700 (emergency) will cause this code to flash on every radar screen within range. It will back up your distress call or may alert controllers even if your radio call is not received, remember VHF range is limited by line of sight.

FURTHER READING: APM VOLUME 6, OPERATIONAL PROCEDURES, CHAPTER 6 — EMERGENCY & PRECAUTIONARY LANDINGS

END OF EXPLANATIONS PAPER 2

1. Unless otherwise prescribed by an appropriate authority, "Night" is between:

   a. The end of morning civil twilight and the beginning of evening civil twilight

   b. The end of evening civil twilight and the beginning of morning civil twilight

   c. The end of evening civil twilight and the end of morning civil twilight

   d. The beginning of morning civil twilight and the end of evening civil twilight

2. A runway is described as "damp" if:

   a. Significant standing water more than 3 mm deep is visible

   b. The surface shows a change in colour due to moisture

   c. There is contamination

   d. Significant standing water less than 3 mm deep is visible

3. What is the ICAO definition of "flight time"?

   a. The time between engine start and engine shut down

   b. The time between taking-off and landing

   c. The time from any person boarding the aircraft with the intention of flight until all persons have disembarked

   d. The time from when an aircraft first moves under its own power with the intention of taking off, until it finally comes to rest after landing

4. You encounter the following low level windshear on final approach: at 1,000 feet a 10 knot headwind component changes to a 30 knot headwind component. What will the effect be on your aircraft's air speed?

   a. The air speed will remain the same

   b. The air speed will increase rapidly

   c. The air speed will increase slowly

   d. The air speed will reduce rapidly

5. The most likely initial consequence of encountering a microburst would be:

   a. A decrease in air speed

   b. Calm air

   c. An increase in air speed

   d. An increased rate of descent

6. A flashing red light directed from the ground to an aircraft in the air means:

   a. Cleared to land

   b. Do not land, aerodrome closed. Go to another aerodrome

   c. Land at this aerodrome, after receiving a steady green light

   d. Do not land, wait for permission

7. In the event of having to ditch, when light winds are present a pilot should aim to:

   a. Touchdown into the swell

   b. Touchdown parallel to the swell, ideally on a crest

   c. Touchdown parallel to the swell, ideally in a trough

   d. Touchdown into wind ignoring the direction of the swell

8. Operations from a contaminated runway:

   a. Are not permitted

   b. Will not affect the performance or handling characteristics of the aircraft

   c. Require written permission

   d. Should be avoided if at all possible

9. When operating at a controlled aerodrome, holding points:

    a. May be crossed as long as a good look out is maintained

    b. Are painted yellow and have blue stop bar lights

    c. May only be crossed with ATC clearance and consist of yellow solid and broken lines

    d. Are there to help you navigate around the airport

10. Which of the following meteorological phenomena may lead to windshear?

    a. Only thunderstorms

    b. Occluded fronts, rain, microbursts and virga

    c. Thunderstorms, temperature inversions, fog and virga

    d. Thunderstorms, frontal passage, marked temperature inversions, virga, microbursts and strong winds

11. Wake turbulence:

    a. Is most hazardous in light or cross wind conditions

    b. Is most hazardous in strong wind

    c. Caused by wing tip vorticies which will drift upwards from the aircraft generating them

    d. Caused by wing tip vorticies which converge from the tip

12. Which of the following statements are correct? When flying a single engine aircraft over water, lifejackets:

    i.   Should be worn by the pilot

    ii.   Should be worn by all occupants of the aircraft

    iii.   Should be carried in the aircraft, one for each occupant of the aircraft

    iv.   Should be inflated as the aircraft touches down

    v.   Should be inflated only when outside of the aircraft

    vi.   Should be worn inflated by all occupants

    a. (ii) and (v)

    b. (vi)

    c. (iii) and (iv)

    d. (ii) and (iv)

13. Engine fire on start is most likely to be caused by:

    a. Over-priming the engine

    b. A malfunction in one of the cylinders

    c. Over use of the starter motor, its failure to disconnect

    d. Charring of the HT leads

14. A cabin fire is often accompanied by acrid smelling smoke. In light aircraft:

    a. It is always caused by exhaust gases leaking into the cabin

    b. It will not be serious enough to warrant a diversion

    c. Electrical malfunction is the most likely cause

    d. A fire in the engine compartment, forward of the bulkhead, is the most likely cause

15. At a controlled aerodrome an illuminated red stop bar:

    a. May be crossed at the discretion of the pilot

    b. May be crossed as long as the pilot holds short of the runway itself

    c. Must not be crossed, ATC will give clearance to enter the runway and simultaneously deselect the stop bar

    d. Must not be crossed, the FISO or AGCS Operator will give clearance to enter the runway and simultaneously deselect the stop bar

16. Following a forced landing, subject to the particular circumstances and the procedures in the aircraft's emergency checklist, which of the following are correct in relation to evacuating the aircraft?

i.   Passengers should be evacuated downwind of the aircraft

ii.   The evacuation should wait until ATC or the Fire Service give authorisation

iii. Passengers should be evacuated upwind of the aircraft

iv.   The aircraft's systems should be left on to facilitate its removal

v.   The fire extinguisher and first aid kit should be taken if possible

vi.   The aircraft's systems should be shut down to make the aircraft safe

a.   (i), (ii) and (v)

b.   (ii), (iv) and (vi)

c.   (i), (v) and (vi)

d.   (iii), (v) and (vi)

END OF OPERATIONAL PROCEDURES PAPER 3

No.	A	B	C	D
1		X		
2		X		
3				X
4		X		
5			X	
6		X		
7		X		
8				X
9			X	
10				X
11	X			
12	X			
13	X			
14			X	
15			X	
16				X

CORRECT ANSWERS:	PERCENTAGES			
12	13	14	15	16
75%	81%	88%	94%	100%

OPERATIONAL PROCEDURES
PAPER 3: EXPLANATIONS

1. **(Answer: B)** Night is the period between the end of evening civil twilight and the beginning of morning civil twilight, or such other period as may be prescribed by the appropriate authority.

NOTE: IN THE UK NIGHT IS DEFINED AS 30 MINUTES AFTER SUNSET UNTIL 30 MINUTES BEFORE SUNRISE.

FURTHER READING: APM VOLUME 6, OPERATIONAL PROCEDURES, CHAPTER 1 – OPERATION OF AIRCRAFT

2. **(Answer: B)** "Damp" means that the surface shows a change in colour due to moisture.

WATER CONTAMINATION ON RUNWAYS:

REPORTING TERM	RUNWAY SURFACE CONDITION	NOTES
Dry	The surface is not affected by water, slush, snow, or ice.	Not usually reported to pilots.
Damp	The surface shows a change in colour due to moisture.	
Wet	The surface is soaked but no significant patches of standing water are visible.	Standing water is considered to exist when water on the runway surface is deeper than 3 mm. Patches of standing water covering more than 25% of the assessed area will be reported as WATER PATCHES.
Water Patches	Significant patches of standing water are visible.	Water patches will be reported when more than 25% of the assessed area is covered by water more than 3mm deep.
Flooded	Extensive patches of standing water are visible.	Flooded will be reported when more than 50% of the assessed area is covered by water more than 3mm deep.

The runway surface is assessed and reported to pilots in thirds – for example it may be described as being "wet/wet/damp".

FURTHER READING: APM VOLUME 6, OPERATIONAL PROCEDURES, CHAPTER 7 – CONTAMINATED RUNWAYS

3. **(Answer: D)** The ICAO definition of "flight time" is that time from when an aircraft first moves under its own power with the intention of taking off, until it finally comes to rest after landing.

FURTHER READING: APM VOLUME 6, OPERATIONAL PROCEDURES, CHAPTER 1 – OPERATION OF AIRCRAFT

4. **(Answer: B)** The airspeed will increase suddenly. If the approach speed was 80 knots IAS, with a 10 knot headwind the ground speed would be 70 knots. Passing through the shear line results in a sudden increase in the headwind, because of inertia the ground speed will change little, however the air speed will now be 110 knots. The increase in airspeed would lead to a deviation above the desired glidepath.

WINDSHEAR INCREASED HEADWIND - ENERGY GAIN

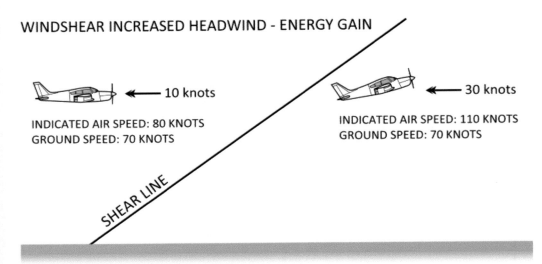

← 10 knots

INDICATED AIR SPEED: 80 KNOTS
GROUND SPEED: 70 KNOTS

← 30 knots

INDICATED AIR SPEED: 110 KNOTS
GROUND SPEED: 70 KNOTS

SHEAR LINE

Windshear is defined as: Variations in the wind vector along the flight path of an aircraft with a pattern, intensity and duration that will displace an aircraft abruptly from its intended flight path such that substantial control input and action is required to correct it. Low altitude windshear is a particular hazard, that is windshear encountered along the final approach path, runway, the take-off or the initial climb-out paths.

FURTHER READING: APM VOLUME 6, OPERATIONAL PROCEDURES, CHAPTER 4 – WINDSHEAR AND MICROBURST

5. **(Answer: C)** The most likely initial consequence of encountering a microburst would be an increase in air speed.

A microburst is very localised but extremely powerful area of descending. Normally microbursts are associated with thunderstorms or similar convective activity and are associated with areas of heavy rain. However, microbursts are also associated with areas of "virga", areas where rain is falling from cloud but evaporating before it reaches the ground.

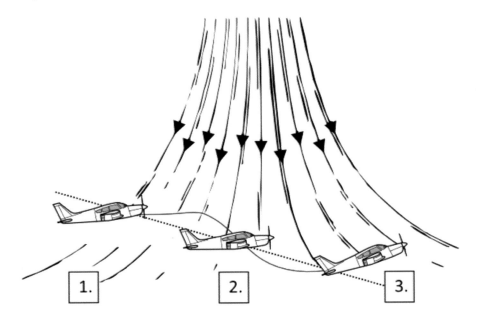

The likely sequence of events during a microburst encounter associated with convective activity is:

1. Energy Gain:
   - Increased headwind
   - Increasing airspeed
   - Reduced rate of descent
   - Tending to become high with regard to desired flight path

2. Energy Loss:
   - Reducing headwind and downdraught
   - Reducing airspeed
   - Increasing rate of descent
   - Tending to become high with regard to desired flight path

3. Energy Loss:
   - Increased tailwind
   - Reducing airspeed

A microburst involves intense downdraughts and possibly severe windshear, if on approach a missed approach is the most sensible course of action and an encounter during take-off could be equally as hazardous.

FURTHER READING: APM VOLUME 6, OPERATIONAL PROCEDURES, CHAPTER 4 – WINDSHEAR AND MICROBURST

6. **(Answer: B)** A flashing red light directed from the ground to an aircraft in the air means "Do not land, aerodrome closed. Go to another aerodrome".

RED LIGHT SIGNALS	TO AIRCRAFT IN THE AIR	TO AIRCRAFT ON THE GROUND
	Do not land. Aerodrome Closed. (Go to another aerodrome)	Move clear of the landing area.
	Do not land. Give way to other aircraft and continue circling.	Stop.
	Do not land. Wait for permission.	
GREEN LIGHT SIGNALS	**TO AIRCRAFT IN THE AIR**	**TO AIRCRAFT ON THE GROUND**
	Cleared to land. If pilot is satisfied that no collision risk exists.	Cleared for take off, if pilot is satisfied that no collision risk exists.
	Return to this aerodrome and wait for permission to land.	Cleared to taxi on the manoeuvring area. If pilot is satisfied that no collision risk exists.
	Land at this aerodrome after receiving a steady green light.	Return to starting point on the aerodrome.

FURTHER READING: APM VOLUME 6, OPERATIONAL PROCEDURES, CHAPTER 2 – NOISE ABATEMENT

7.   **(Answer: B)** When planning a ditching the conventional wisdom is that the swell direction is more important than wind direction. From approximately 2,000 feet, the direction of the swell should be clear and your aim should be to touchdown parallel to the line of the swell and ideally to land along the crest.

     If spray and spume can be seen on the surface of the water, then there is a strong surface wind . In this case it may be better to plan to land into wind, rather than along the swell. The best course of action is to aim for the crest again or, if that is not possible, into the downslope.

     See table on page 19.

     FURTHER READING: APM VOLUME 6, OPERATIONAL PROCEDURES, CHAPTER 6 — EMERGENCY & PRECAUTIONARY LANDINGS

8.   **(Answer: D)** AIC Pink 126 advises that: "the use of a contaminated runway should be avoided if at all possible. A short delay in take-off or a short hold before landing can sometimes be sufficient to remove the contaminated runway risk. If necessary a longer delay or diversion to an aerodrome with a more suitable runway should be considered".

     AIC Pink 126 Risks and factors associated with operations on runways affected by snow, slush or water.

     FURTHER READING: APM VOLUME 6, OPERATIONAL PROCEDURES, CHAPTER 7 — CONTAMINATED RUNWAYS

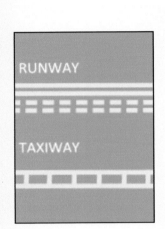

9.   **(Answer: C)** When operating at a controlled aerodrome, holding points may only be crossed with ATC clearance and consist of yellow solid and broken lines.

     The holding point closest to the runway will consist of solid and broken yellow lines and this may only be crossed after receiving ATC permission to do so. Intermediate holding points are of a "ladder" style, and you may also be asked to stop at any of these in you taxi clearance.

     At large airports holding points may be reinforced with red stop bar lights. An illuminated red stop bar must NEVER be crossed. ATC will deselect the lights at the same time as giving permission to enter the runway.

     FURTHER READING: APM VOLUME 6, OPERATIONAL PROCEDURES, CHAPTER 2 — NOISE ABATEMENT

10. **The meteorological** circumstances where windshear may be encountered include:
     *   Thunderstorms (both from the gust front and microburst),
     *   The passage of a front,
     *   A marked temperature inversion,
     *   A turbulent boundary layer
     *   Mcrobursts
     *   Virga
     *   Strong wind

     Additionally, topography or buildings can create substantial local windshear effects.

     FURTHER READING: APM VOLUME 6, OPERATIONAL PROCEDURES, CHAPTER 4 — WINDSHEAR AND MICROBURST

11. **(Answer: A)** Wake turbulence is most hazardous in light or cross wind conditions.

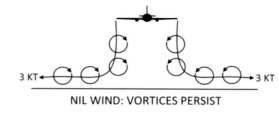

NIL WIND: VORTICES PERSIST

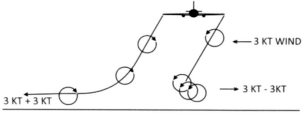

LIGHT CROSS WIND: HOLDS UPWIND
VORTEX IN PLACE

Conversely, the low level turbulence, associated with stronger wind conditions, will accelerate vortex decay.

FURTHER READING: APM VOLUME 6, OPERATIONAL PROCEDURES, CHAPTER 4 – WINDSHEAR AND MICROBURST

12. **(Answer: A)** The advice held in a CAA General Aviation Safety Sense leaflet recommends that when flying beyond gliding distance of land life jackets should be worn by all occupants. Additionally, passengers must be briefed that life jackets must be inflated only when they are outside of the aircraft.

FURTHER READING: APM VOLUME 6, OPERATIONAL PROCEDURES, CHAPTER 1 – OPERATION OF AIRCRAFT

13. **(Answer: A)** The most likely cause of an engine fire during start is over-priming. This is done either over using the primer, or if the aircraft has an accelerator pump in its carburettor, repeated "pumping" of the throttle lever. Whatever the cause, the result is that excess fuel can collect in the induction system and potentially be a fire hazard.

FURTHER READING: APM VOLUME 6, OPERATIONAL PROCEDURES, CHAPTER 3 – FIRE OR SMOKE

14. **(Answer: C)** Any discussion here regarding emergency procedures is for guidance only. The Emergency Checklist and Pilot's Operating Handbook will contain instructions and procedures to be followed specific to your aircraft type, and particular circumstances will vary.

In light aircraft cabin fires during a flight are rare, the most likely cause is a malfunction with an electrical component.

Electrical fires are characterised by an acrid smell possibly accompanied by a white smoke.

If the source can be identified:
Switch off the device
Pull the circuit breaker or fuse

If the source cannot be identified:
Shut down all electrics using the master switch

In both cases consider a diversion or forced landing according to circumstances.

FURTHER READING: APM VOLUME 6, OPERATIONAL PROCEDURES, CHAPTER 3 – FIRE OR SMOKE

15. **(Answer: C)** A controlled aerodrome is one where Air Traffic Control is provided. Where installed, a red stop bar is located at the holding point nearest to the runway. An illuminated red stop bar must not be crossed, ATC will give clearance to enter the runway and simultaneously deselect the lights.

FURTHER READING: APM VOLUME 6, OPERATIONAL PROCEDURES, CHAPTER 2 – NOISE ABATEMENT

---

16. **(Answer: D)** Any discussion here regarding emergency procedures is for guidance only. The Emergency Checklist and Pilot's Operating Handbook will contain instructions and procedures to be followed specific to your aircraft type, and particular circumstances will vary.

The following are generally universal when evacuating an aircraft following a forced landing:
- Aircraft systems should be shut down.
- Passengers evacuated a safe distance upwind of the aircraft, away from any flames or smoke.
- Time permitting, the fire extinguisher and first aid kit should be taken.

FURTHER READING: APM VOLUME 6, OPERATIONAL PROCEDURES, CHAPTER 6 – EMERGENCY & PRECAUTIONARY LANDINGS

END OF EXPLANATIONS PAPER 3

INTENTIONALLY BLANK

ANSWER SHEETS

PAPER NO.				
	A	B	C	D
1				
2				
3				
4				
5				
6				
7				
8				
9				
10				
11				
12				
13				
14				
15				
16				

PAPER NO.				
	A	B	C	D
1				
2				
3				
4				
5				
6				
7				
8				
9				
10				
11				
12				
13				
14				
15				
16				

PAPER NO.				
	A	B	C	D
1				
2				
3				
4				
5				
6				
7				
8				
9				
10				
11				
12				
13				
14				
15				
16				

PAPER NO.				
	A	B	C	D
1				
2				
3				
4				
5				
6				
7				
8				
9				
10				
11				
12				
13				
14				
15				
16				

PAPER NO.				
	A	B	C	D
1				
2				
3				
4				
5				
6				
7				
8				
9				
10				
11				
12				
13				
14				
15				
16				

PAPER NO.				
	A	B	C	D
1				
2				
3				
4				
5				
6				
7				
8				
9				
10				
11				
12				
13				
14				
15				
16				

PAPER NO.				
	A	**B**	**C**	**D**
1				
2				
3				
4				
5				
6				
7				
8				
9				
10				
11				
12				
13				
14				
15				
16				

PAPER NO.				
	A	**B**	**C**	**D**
1				
2				
3				
4				
5				
6				
7				
8				
9				
10				
11				
12				
13				
14				
15				
16				

PAPER NO.				
	A	**B**	**C**	**D**
1				
2				
3				
4				
5				
6				
7				
8				
9				
10				
11				
12				
13				
14				
15				
16				

PAPER NO.				
	A	B	C	D
1				
2				
3				
4				
5				
6				
7				
8				
9				
10				
11				
12				
13				
14				
15				
16				

PAPER NO.				
	A	B	C	D
1				
2				
3				
4				
5				
6				
7				
8				
9				
10				
11				
12				
13				
14				
15				
16				

PAPER NO.				
	A	B	C	D
1				
2				
3				
4				
5				
6				
7				
8				
9				
10				
11				
12				
13				
14				
15				
16				